Anna Robbins 25/12/94

POCKET PAINTERS

MONET

1 8 4 0 — 1 9 2 6

CLARKSON POTTER/PUBLISHERS

NEW YORK

Monet

Claude Monet (1840-1926) was born in Paris but grew up at Le Havre, at the mouth of the Seine. Both coast and river, close to which he lived throughout his life, were to play a central role in his artistic development. It was at Le Havre that Monet found his first mentors in the local artist Eugene Boudin, who opened his eyes to the possibilities of painting landscapes in the open air, and the Dutch painter Johan Barthold Jongkind, whose fluent style influenced him profoundly when they painted there together in 1864.

At the studio of Charles Gleyre in Paris, Monet met Sisley, Bazille and Renoir, who were persuaded to join him on painting expeditions to Fontainebleau. By the end of the 1860s, during most of which Monet lived in extreme poverty, he had found that the reaches of the Seine below Paris offered ideal subjects for painting *'directly in front of nature'*, and the stretch between Louveciennes and Bougival, where he and Renoir painted together in 1869, is regarded as the birthplace of Impressionism. Although he had already exhibited several times at the Salon, Monet took part in all the Impressionist exhibitions of the 1870s, and was arguably the central figure of the movement. While he was no theorist, none had greater influence or adhered so consistently to Impressionist precepts.

After seeing out the France-Prussian War in London, where the Thames provided a compelling subject, Monet and his wife Camille lived for most of the decade at Argenteuil. In his river scenes of the period, many of which were painted on the floating studio built for him by the painter Caillebotte, figures and background occupied him less and less as he concentrated on capturing the fleeting effects of light on water.

For many years after Camille's death in 1879 Monet travelled extensively, but returned with ever greater pleasure to his new home at Giverny, to which he had moved in 1883 with Alice Hoschédé, (later to be his second wife), and where he was creating an idyllic garden. In the 1890s, now finally established as an artist and financially secure, Monet took to producing series of studies of the same object – Poplars, Haystacks, Rouen Cathedral, the Thames – in different light and weather conditions. With the completion in 1899 of the water garden at Giverny, he began the series of paintings of waterlilies which occupied him for most of his last 25 years, and in which a lifetime's development is seen to culminate in virtually abstract studies of pure colour. ◢

View of Rouelles

Oil on canvas
1858
46 × 65 cm

This highly proficient study of the lush Normandy countryside, painted when Monet was seventeen, is one of his earliest surviving landscapes. A painting expedition with Boudin a year or so before had been a revelation – *My destiny as a painter was decided.'*

*Women in the
Garden*

Oil on canvas
1866 – 7
256 × 208 cm

Painted outdoors at Ville d'Avray, this
large canvas was intended for the
Salon, where Monet had had a great
success with *Camille* in 1866. Monet's
future wife Camille Doncieux posed
for all four figures, based on Frédéric
Bazille's family, and Monet dug a
trench for the canvas to enable him
to reach the upper part. The painting
was rejected by the Salon, but bought
by Bazille.

The Hôtel Roches-Noires at Trouville

Oil on canvas
1870
81 × 58.5 cm

In the summer of 1870, with France at war with Prussia, Monet was at Trouville on the Normandy coast, producing rapid studies of his new wife on the beach and painting coastal features such as this luxury hotel. The Monets had chosen more modest accommodation for themselves – but still left without paying the bill.

Tulip Fields with the Rijnsburg Windmill

Oil on canvas
1886
65 × 81 cm

Monet first visited Holland in 1871, following his year in England during the Franco-Prussian War, and returned several times in the early 1870's to paint mostly in the area round Zaandam, near Amsterdam. This scene in the tulip fields near Leiden dates from a visit he made in 1886.

Impression, Sunrise

Oil on canvas
1872
48 × 63 cm

Ironically, since Monet did not care greatly for Turner's work, it was this most Turneresque of his paintings which accidentally gave Monet and his friend their identity. At the first group exhibition of 1874, a hostile critic seized on the title, labelling them all 'Impressionists', and the name stuck.

Overleaf – In 1872 Monet and his family moved to Argenteuil, on the Seine, and over the next few years, a time of contentment and relative prosperity, the river and the surrounding countryside inspired some of his most idyllic paintings. This one has much in common with Renoir's *Path through the Long Grass*.

Wild Poppies

Oil on canvas
1873
50 × 65 cm

Argenteuil

Oil on canvas
c. 1875
55 × 65 cm

Much of Monet's time during the
Argenteuil years was spent by or on the
river, in all weathers, applying his
spontaneous technique to the
impressions created by water and
reflections under changing conditions
of light. Impressionist colleagues came
to join him, and the movement would
never know such unity again.

A Woman Reading

Oil on canvas
c.1875
50 × 65.5 cm

Camille Monet posed for this exquisite study in which Monet tackled a subject frequently explored by Renoir: the effect on figures of dappled light through foliage. The Argenteuil idyll was not to last much longer, dire financial difficulty coincided with Camille's illness, and the decade ended in tragedy.

Overleaf – Early in 1877 Monet discovered the poetry of iron, glass and steam at the new St Lazare station. *'This year,'* wrote Emile Zola, *'Monet exhibited some superb station interiors. You can hear the rumbling of the trains as the station engulfs them. You can see the smoke billowing out beneath the vast hangars. That's painting today …'*

The Gare St-Lazare

Oil on canvas
1877
75 × 100 cm

Rue Montorgueil

Oil on canvas
1878
80 × 50 cm

Monet painted this riot of patriotic
colour on 30 June 1878, when the first
Fête Nationale to be celebrated since
the war coincided with the opening of
the World Fair. Broad brush-strokes
capture the waving tricolour flags and
heighten the impression of Paris in
joyous movement.

Spring

Oil on canvas
1886
65 × 81 cm

This is an orchard at Giverny, where Monet had settled in 1883, together with Alice Hoschédé, later his second wife, her children and his own. Monet did not at first find much to catch his eye in the placid landscape, but it grew on him. Soon, in any case, his own garden would provide all the inspiration he needed.

***Woman with a
Parasol, Turned to
the Left***

Oil on canvas
1886
131 × 88 cm

In 1886, possibly in reaction to the
frozen figures of Seurat's *La Grande
Jatte*, Monet undertook a series of
open-air paintings of figures in natural
spontaneous attitudes. This painting,
one of a pair for which Suzanne
Hoschédé posed, is a re-working of an
earlier work, *Promenade*, for which
Camille had posed in 1875.

The Rocks of Belle-Ile

Oil on canvas
1886
63 × 79 cm

In 1886 Monet travelled to south-west Brittany and found entirely new subject-matter on the tiny island of Belle-Ile. Often working in wind and rain, he used deep colours and vigorous brush-strokes to capture the violence of the sea and the ferocity of the granite outcrops.

Antibes

Oil on canvas
1888
65 × 92 cm

On his second Mediterranean trip in
1888, Monet spent four months in the
Cap d'Antibes area, where he tried out
new methods of conveying the brilliant
southern light. This view, with its
almost Japanese serenity, demonstrates
his way of unifying a painting by
using the same colours, in different
proportions, in every area of the
canvas.

Haystack at Sunset,
Frosty Weather

Oil on canvas
1891
65 × 92 cm

In 1890 Monet began the first of
several organized series of painting
of the same subject under subtly
changing conditions. In the
Haystacks series, as in *Poplars* and
Rouen Cathedral, the real subject is the
change itself, observed by comparing
the paintings. A remarkable feature
here is the luminous effect achieved
by the juxtaposition of contrasting
colours.

The Artist's Garden at Giverny

Oil on canvas
1900
81 × 92 cm

Giverny provided Monet with his first real chance to create a floral paradise. He designed the garden along formal lines, but planted so as to create a profusion of colour. *'What I needed most are flowers, always, always.'* He never tired of showing visitors around it – and he painted it over five hundred times.

London, Parliament with the Sun Breaking through Fog

Oil on canvas
1904
81 × 92 cm

At the turn of the century Monet went to London three winters in a row and, out of London fog and Gothic architecture, created some of his most mysterious images. Unable to match the speed with which the mists moved, however, he broke his own rule by finishing them at Giverny. *'It's the result that counts,'* he said.

The Boat at Giverny

Oil on canvas
c.1887
98 × 131 cm

This idyllic study of piscatory elegance reflected in the limpid waters of the Epte was painted in the early days at Giverny. A dozen years later Monet's private water paradise would be completed, with the models that would inspire him for much of his last quarter-century spreading silently across its surface.

The Water-Lily Pond

Oil on canvas
1900
89.5 × 100 cm

Monet designed his tranquil water garden with the help of a Japanese gardener and diverted the little River Ru to fill his initial pond, which he spanned with a Japanese bridge. The pond was later extended, and the bridge festooned with wisteria. It survives today as the focal point of Monet's living memorial.

Water-Lilies

Oil on canvas
1904
90 × 93 cm

Monet always insisted that the
inspiration for his final and most
famous series took him unawares:
I planted my water-lilies for pleasure.
I cultivated them without thinking of
painting them. A landscape does not
get through to you all at once. And then,
suddenly, I had the revelation of the
magic of my pond.'

Published by Clarkson N. Potter, Inc., 201 East 50th Street,
New York, New York 10022. Member of the Crown Publishing Group.

Random House, Inc. New York, Toronto, London, Sydney, Auckland.

CLARKSON N. POTTER, POTTER, and colophon are
trademarks of Clarkson N. Potter, Inc.

Originally published in Great Britain by Pavilion Books Limited in 1994

Manufactured in Italy

ISBN 0-517-59966-X

10   9   8   7   6   5   4   3   2   1

First American Edition

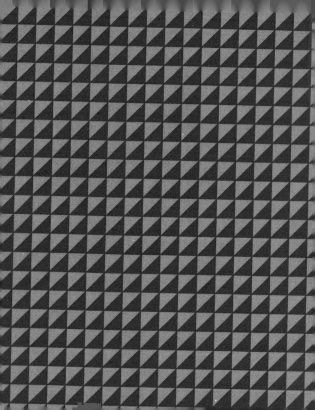